BORN TO JUMP

A Personal Journey of Overcoming Fear and Failures and

Allowing Faith to Lead to a Life of Freedom

L'Tanya Parks

ISBN: 9798985619720

Printed in the United States of America

Cover design by: Avenue K Web Design

Edited by: H.R.S Editorial

Robinson Anderson Publishing

2150 South Central Expressway, Suite 200

McKinney, TX 75070

info@rapublishingco.com

DEDICATION

This memoir is dedicated to my mother, Erma Hinton, who might not have understood my journey, but loved me all the way through it. Mom, I watched you sacrifice your body and soul for the sake of family, and that left an imprint on my heart forever. Thank you for loving me unconditionally.

I also dedicate this book to my children, Taylore and Sterling, who allowed me to love them with so much "Meraki." God knew I would go to the ends of the earth for you both and come out unscathed.

FOREWORD

Few people have impressed me as much as L'Tanya Parks, and I feel incredibly blessed to know her. Though not towering in stature, she has a presence and warmth that fills a room the second she enters it. She radiates in any space she occupies. She is always the light. Though these pages are filled with some of the darkest experiences and toughest times of her life, she wanted to tell her story and let it serve as an inspiration to other people to push forward with courage, faith, and tenacity. She is on a constant quest to live her life freely and happily without the weight of anyone else's expectations or judgments. That spirit of freedom and levity is one of the reasons she admires butterflies so much. Most importantly, L'Tanya believes that everyone must seek to be like the butterfly in spirit – to be free of those things they feel keep them stuck with a life that isn't quite what they wanted or imagined for themselves. As she tells her stories about her life's journeys, I hope they motivate you (as they have me and countless others) to pursue the freedom and happiness we all so long to achieve and live more abundant, joyful, and faithful lives.

The cocktails? Well…they are a bonus! Cheers!

– *Stacy Fitzgerald-Redd*

PREFACE

Sometimes you don't realize how pivotal an event is until you're behind it. Other times, you can tell that something has shifted that is truly significant in the midst of it. Even if you don't know how events will unfold, you realize that something epic is afoot. A birth, a loss, an achievement, a marriage, children with challenges, and a breakup can change everything. Amid these occurrences, it is essential to pause, process your emotions, and weigh your available options.

People often determine that their options are few and that there are fixed elements of their lives that they cannot alter. *What I have learned is that the opposite is true.* You can change the trajectory of your life IF you embrace your ability to do one simple thing that alters your view, changes your location and energy, or shifts everything in your current life. And that is *JUMP.*

Jumps are significant changes that one needs to avoid self-destruction and bring an abundance and clarity that wouldn't be possible in stillness. I was at a point in my life where I was stuck in a routine that seemed predictable, safe, and stable but didn't provide a sense of anticipation when I came home from work. My life was stifled, and my spirit was crying out for freedom. But what did that mean? What is freedom?

There are three types of freedom[1]. The first kind is "freedom from," as in freedom from the constraints of society. The second is "freedom to," which refers to the freedom to do what we want. The third is "freedom to be," or in other words, freedom not just to do what we want, but a freedom to be who we were meant to be. I craved all of them and wanted to ascend to something new.

Every day, I felt like something was missing, like a jigsaw puzzle with a gaping hole in it left by a missing piece. I knew I wanted to find that piece. The thing about puzzles is that often, people do them together – they're a team sport. But I knew I'd have to find my piece alone because whatever this internal feeling was, only I could make sense of it. Albert Einstein said, "The one who follows the crowd will usually get no further than the crowd. The one who walks alone is likely to find himself in places no one has ever been." I wanted to be in the place within my spirit that I had never been. I had dreams of traveling to different countries and experiencing other cultures. I was always intrigued by foreign customs, beliefs, and foods from people around the world. Growing up in a military community aided in this thought process. Oscar Wilde said, "Life imitates art far more than art imitates life." As human beings, we are absolutely inspired by what we see around us, including television, movies,

---

[1] Wikipedia.

and social media. I decided I did not have to follow any rules - I wanted to create a life free of whatever the norm was and allow my spirit to lead me.

Identifying and then tapping into your gifts and talents when you jump will create a pathway for you to experience a more joyful, abundant life. My talents include being empathetic and serving others, and I expressed that servant spirit in hospitality. Bartending was the form I chose after my children were grown. I've always loved serving others and meeting new people. Bartending not only taught me about other people but also about myself and the world.

Before getting into bartending, my previous careers had been in education, business, and entrepreneurship. I was part owner of an afterschool program with the former member of an R & B group, where he taught children how to play music. After teaching, I ventured into the mortgage industry and became a branch manager. I was an explorer and tried so many things. This allowed me to cultivate my free spirit.

As a bartender, my greatest skill was being a travel and tourism advisor for my clients. In this book, you can think of me as a tour guide as this is a manual to help you create a life of adventure for yourself. I hope that in telling my story of how and why I skip, jump, and sometimes even leap, I will inspire you to do the same, even if it means you will have to take new risks (newsflash – you will have them anyway) or face the unknown (the start of every day brings the unknown). In a nod to my bartending craft, I also offer a cocktail that represents a phase of my story in every chapter for you to enjoy.

So, exactly what are skips, jumps, and leaps? Skips are normal routines with anticipation of advancing from your everyday routine. Jumps are significant changes or advances in your story. Leaps are huge upheavals, and while they might sound undesirable or negative, sometimes major upheavals provide the opportunity to live your purpose and create a boundless life. Throughout these dramatic movements in your story, you must have *faith to keep moving forward.* I believe that if you use your unique and God-given talents in your new endeavors, you will create a more fulfilled, joyful life, renew your focus and energy, and cultivate more rewarding relationships and connections. Please keep in mind that whether you are skipping, leaping, or jumping, any of these actions can alter the way you think and make decisions moving forward.

I hope to inspire you to create yours.

Contents

1

LEARNING TO SKIP

Shirley Temple Recipe

Sprite
Grenadine
Maraschino Cherry
Crushed ice

During the first two years of life, the Centers for Disease Control and Prevention (CDC) explains that "Children reach milestones in how to play, learn, speak, behave, and move (like walking, skipping, and jumping)." Those learned actions stay with us as we mature and are engraved in our minds and hearts. For example, when a baby sees someone talking to them face-to-face, they want to emulate the same jester. I learned very early about traveling due to my father choosing a military career, and like a baby talking, traveling became a natural and automatic movement for me.

I was blessed to have been born into a loving, nurturing environment and a tight-knit family. My parents had five daughters, and I was the youngest. Because my father was an airman in the U.S. Air Force, we lived in many places, and I was born in Tokyo, Japan. My story is unique from the beginning. I was called a "dirty baby," meaning one that was not born in a hospital. My mother told me she was unable to make it to the hospital because I "came too fast." Growing up and hearing that story always made me feel special and different, and while most people would have been offended to be called that, I didn't think it was offensive at all. I can't explain why.

During the first few years of my life, we lived in Japan, but I don't remember any of it because my family and I moved to Maine at an early age. Maine was where Daddy's new duty station was, and he was the consummate military man who was comfortable with traveling both professionally and personally. Daddy was also an adventurous family man who loved nothing more than a good family trip and our excursions, which were mostly by car and always had a theme. He always played games with us as well as a variety of music during our long road trips. He even taught us to sing military cadences. Those trips were the best!

As the stereotypical "youngest in the family," I was always treated as special by my father, mother, and sisters. I even had a special nickname. My father referred to me as "That Baby" while my mother nicknamed me "Tears." I must admit I was spoiled rotten as a child (although, in my opinion, only food spoils). Being the baby of the bunch, Daddy felt I needed protection, and because of it, I always had the best seat in the car - in the front, positioned directly between the King, my Daddy, and the Queen, my Mom. It was in this cocoon of protection and adoration that I experienced a childhood that didn't necessarily shower me with material things but was constantly rooted in love, respect, and joy.

My father was a hard-working man and a meticulous planner and entrepreneur. At 15, he opened a corner store in his neighborhood. Later, he also opened a janitorial business, which he turned into a family affair. I didn't realize as a kid that we were cleaning government buildings because he made everything such an adventurous experience. He always had a fun story to tell and would make even the most menial tasks enjoyable. Daddy was great that way, and he is where my sisters and I got our spirits.

The argument will always be made that nature, rather than nurture, is the most powerful force in determining who we become as people. But I don't believe that. I look at family as the ground that ultimately cultivates us into the people we will become, for better or worse. I think how we're nurtured - what feeds us and inspires joy in us - can be even more powerful in shaping who we become. We can't change what we're born into, but we can change at any time what surrounds us, our relationships to those surroundings, and how we interact with our environments to cultivate the lives we want.

Some of my earliest memories of my father are ones that to this day, put a smile on my face and fill me with happiness. Daddy was a man of strong faith, a loving husband, and a doting father to his girls. He loved to entertain almost as much as Mom did, and he especially loved the holidays. He started a family tradition of the whole family singing Christmas Carols, one line at a time, on Christmas Day. His favorite was "The Twelve Days of Christmas." I always had to sing the "5 Golden Rings" line; Daddy wanted it that way, and so it was. For as far back as I can remember, we did this every Christmas as a family. It became a tradition. He always had a way of making me feel, even among my other siblings, that I was the only child. My sisters even had a standing joke that I was an only child (with four sisters). He understood what being the baby was like since he was the youngest of his family.

My father's mission in life was to ensure that his girls grew up knowing that they were loved and would always be home among family. He and Mom were traditional in every sense and were determined that my sisters and I would be raised to be rooted in our faith, to appreciate education, to live happily, and to cultivate relationships with people who brought positive energy, joy, and laughter into our lives. It was a wonderful way to experience childhood and a great foundation to help shape us into the people we would become.

Both Daddy's and Mom's families were originally from Columbus, Georgia. I remember as a kid taking long drives during the summer from Maine to Columbus. In addition to those many summer excursions, we also visited extended family in Detroit. We would pack our bags and hit the road early in the morning for the hours-long drive with my four older sisters in the back seat and me settled snugly between Dad, who always was the chauffeur, and Mom, our planner and comforter. He purchased a CB Radio and told everyone to come up with handles to talk on it. His name was "The International Skipper." My mother was "Foxy Grandma." Daddy unknowingly cultivated the travel bug in me from an early age. My job on these trips was extremely important: I was the DJ tasked with making sure we had good music to listen to. When a station faded out, I would find another one with familiar soul music or gospel to keep us entertained and that we could sing along to. *There is no better feeling in the world than that of being protected and loved this way.*

My father knew the route to his hometown very well, having driven it all of his adult life, and yet he made each trip new because he'd tell different jokes or stories of when he grew up. He never let boredom or routine overtake us and would allow us to take turns with music and game choices. Mom would make little lunches and snacks for the ride to tide us over to the next meal, and we'd always stop early enough to swim at a hotel and have a great dinner. My sister Teresa and I are two years apart, so we did a lot of things together. I shared a room with her until I was 16 years old. She and I would order Shirley Temples with our dinner. We thought that was a big deal because we weren't allowed to drink soda any other time. I would give her my cherry, though. One of Daddy's famous sayings was, "It only cost a few pennies more to go first class." I use this phrase right now for my Travel Agency company name. He believed in quality and was a first-class man. These cherished memories will forever be etched in my mind.

Looking back on those experiences as an adult, I know without question that they were instrumental in shaping me as a person. I now know that no matter where I was, at home or on the road to some known or unknown destination, I would feel guided, protected, and encouraged to change the channels when I didn't like a song or when the music simply faded. It was a happy existence that instilled a sense of self-confidence, decisiveness, and anticipation in me to always believe that over the next bend, or in the next town, there would always be something new to experience – whether a new song, a new tourist attraction, or a new type of food. Most importantly, I knew there would always be an adventure!

Those road trips shaped my worldview and inspired a love of travel in me that has lasted a lifetime. I'm currently still riding across the country and seeing things with new eyes. I learned early that a change of scenery or routine could bring a new perspective, new treats, and a perfect sunset in a hundred different towns. The discovery, wonder, freedom, and thrill of traveling were feelings that I grew to crave rather than be nervous about, even though at some points of my life, that sense of awe and adventure was dormant. I was always aware that something new and different may not be such a bad thing and could mean new blessings and opportunities. This explained how I came to understand that the importance of something as simple as a road trip can ultimately serve as a metaphor for life. The reality is that your journey can be both rooted in who and what you know (in terms of the people who center you) and global (concerning the geography and culture that nourishes you and feeds your soul). This is how I learned to skip!

Skipping is like swimming. Children are afraid of the water until their parents gently lead them out and teach them how to swim. This is what Daddy did for me. He eased us out into the world until we knew that we could skip, leap, and jump on our own so that we would never be afraid to leave the safety of the shore.

However, as much as my parents, especially my father, loved to travel, the reason that those trips to his home were so important was that they were about family. One of my favorite novels, Anna Karenina by Leo Tolstoy, starts with this sentence: "Happy families are all alike; each unhappy family is unhappy in its own way." I have found that happy families all adhere to a set of values, beliefs, and very similar practices, even across cultures. Yes, all families are different, but there are many commonalities among families who grow up close and connected. There's always laughter, food, good drinks, and faith involved. Those things shaped my early years and have been a part of my existence my whole life.

When you grow up within such a family, you learn that there are people who always root for you, look forward to seeing you, and are eager to see you flourish. Sometimes, those people are related to you by blood, and sometimes, they are the family you choose – friends who span the decades and stick with you through all of life's circumstances and events. They will be the first to go with you to pick up that passport application and even fill one out alongside you. They will go with you on that adventure or encourage you to change your environment and the energy that you are surrounded by. They will encourage you to truly live.

What are some early childhood memories that played an important role in who you are and what decisions you made?

2

A Firm Foundation

Old Fashioned

½ teaspoon sugar
3 dashes of bitters
1 teaspoon of water
2 oz bourbon
Orange peel garnish

As I was maturing, I concluded that what Daddy meant by substance included goals, ambition, and the ability to achieve their desired life. Education was a key part of that, but more importantly, Daddy wanted to know that any boy interested in one of his girls could and would provide what we were accustomed to. As he instilled his value for "substance" in us, we learned that character was essential. He was protective, yes, but more than that, both he and Mom taught us self-reliance and self-esteem. Their teachings were designed to ensure that we would view our worth as more than that of a single element of our being, regardless of our education, career, or spouse. It was the totality of our character and being that defined us, as well as the impact we sought to make on our world, no matter how small or expansive in scope our world was. I can compare my parents' values to how an Old Fashioned is prepared. This cocktail is one of the oldest mixed drinks. It became en vogue after Prohibition around the late 1800's. The ingredients in this timeless drink allow the whiskey to shine. It's made gently, usually stirred the way our parents nurtured and cared for my sisters and I as if each of us were their only child. Along with values such as faith, love, and the insistence that we show hospitality to each other, as well as others, they created a priceless childhood for us.

Of all my father's daughters, I was the one who never thought about being married. I always had a free spirit. Always. I never really expected that to change. Then in college, I was introduced to Jowell by a mutual friend. At first, I never noticed him and couldn't believe I had classes with him. But later, I invited him to a party that I was having at my apartment and was surprised when he and his friend showed up. Things moved quickly from that point, and ten months after we met, we were married while we were both still students at Virginia State University. The reason that we married so fast was because he was in the ROTC and would soon be stationed in Germany. It's funny how we make so many decisions when we are young adults. "Young love" can make you take jumps and leaps you never imagined taking!

I knew Jowell would eventually be a full-time soldier commissioned in the Army, which meant that we would travel the globe. It was at his first duty station in Germany where our daughter, Taylore, was born. When we returned to the states after Jowell was deployed to Desert Storm, we moved to Kentucky, where our son, Sterling, was born. After leaving Kentucky, we moved to Poquoson, Virginia, and I enrolled at Norfolk State University and completed my degree. Jowell was offered a great opportunity from the Army to get his Master's Degree so he could teach at The West Point Military Academy. Since my father was a military man, the transition to being the wife of one was second nature. I was accustomed to picking up and moving. Every time you move with the military, it becomes easier and easier to leave and start anew. As a matter of fact, your body develops an internal clock, and you start anticipating and looking forward to moving. *This is why jumping is second nature to me.* It also makes you look at life from a much different perspective, almost like an evangelist.

Evangelists are committed to the act of public preaching and the intention of spreading the word of God. That's exactly what you do as a military family – you meet new people and enjoy getting to know them and spending time with them. You share your faith, strength, hopes, customs, and most of all, your love. Sometimes you stay connected with the people you meet along life's paths, and sometimes, it's only for that season in life. I truly believe that everyone we meet is not an accident.

Getting married and having children are both major changes – you literally leap into adulthood. However, my parents prepared me well for this change and responsibility. Plus, given that Daddy considered military service to be an especially important sign of substance in a man, he fell in love with Jowell instantly. He always wanted a son, and that's exactly what he became. When our kids were born, this added a branch to the family tree that brought the new grandparents joy and pride. It was beautiful to witness, and I loved that we could do that for my parents – to meet and exceed their expectations. I was proud of that. Daddy loved that Jowell was in the military like he was. He respected that. When it was our turn to move and take road trips, I took on Daddy's role. I made it fun and copied the same habits and rituals I had for Taylore and Sterling. They even learned military cadences just like we did. There were times when Mom and Daddy joined us and we traveled together often.

Jowell got out of the military in 2000, and we moved to Virginia and into the house with my mom and dad. By then, Daddy was the full-time pastor of a church in Falmouth, Virginia. Oh, how I looked forward to coming home to visit and see my father in that capacity! It was a small, country church with wooden floors. We sometimes liked to surprise him. His eyes would light up when we all walked in. I took delight in doing that. I can still hear the sounds of feet tapping while the organ was playing. It was a traditional Baptist church. Daddy always loved to hear me stand up and "testify." The choir director knew when he saw my face, he would have to sing one of my favorite songs – I had so many. It was such a joy to see my father giving hope to the congregation. What great memories!

Daddy got sick suddenly. After a series of doctor visits, we learned that he had Leukemia and that treatment would include chemotherapy and radiation. There was no guarantee that this would prolong his life. I was heartbroken and scared at the prospect of losing my protector and my biggest cheerleader. I couldn't imagine him not being around. To this day, Daddy's passing seems like a scene out of a Spike Lee movie, when the main character floats by on a conveyor belt until they are suddenly out of sight. That's exactly what happened when Daddy died. The world as I knew it stopped, and I floated through the motions. I was stuck on the conveyor belt of life. I felt lost.

Strangely, the 30 days preceding his death were some of the best days of my life. I was fortunate enough to go see him every morning and spend time with him. Daddy's illness often gave us a chance to talk. He used much of this time to prepare me for the possibility that he might not be around – that he might lose his battle with Leukemia. Though it was difficult to have those initial conversations about his frailty and the uncertainty of his treatment, I was also grateful that he trusted me to be mature enough to talk about the finality of death without becoming overly emotional.

He told me to be there for Mommy, who'd been his best friend and love for more than 45 years, and specifically where to find his banking and insurance information so that she wouldn't have to handle those things alone. He reminded me repeatedly that it was okay to be sad but not discouraged because he would be going home to be with God when he passed. One month later, he was gone.

Losing my Daddy was a jump – my first jump. A jump that hurt and left me with scars. It was a jump that changed my life forever. The deep sense of loss wasn't necessarily easier because he had told me that his death was impending, but the sound of his voice – strong, optimistic, with laughter at the end, comforted me as I dealt with the profound sense of abandonment. My dad had even written his own eulogy. He told us if God healed him, he would win and he said if God called him home, he would win. He said, "either way, it's a win-win situation," and that was what the pastor preached at his funeral.

I feel in many ways that my father's death was one of those pivotal moments that led to something momentous. Though I was 35 when he passed, it was the first time in my life that I realized that life was short and meant to be meaningful and joyful. It was by far the most painful experience I ever had to deal with in my life. The pain of losing him blunted my emotions and led me to make some regrettable decisions, such as not keeping my children's and family's needs first. Nevertheless, there was also self-reflection and growth that came from that tremendously difficult time.

What I learned during this period is that the things that make you happy are worth pursuing and that living life with a sense of gratitude and awe for our gifts and blessings must be part of our daily existence. Being grounded in your faith and belief in a higher power will see you through any situation. It doesn't mean that you won't have difficult times and challenges, but it does mean that you'll be able to see them through with the knowledge that you don't fight any of your battles unprepared. You have talents, and even when you feel alone, you have God.

It is with that new epiphany that I proceeded into the next phase – and prepared to jump.

3

FORCED TO JUMP

Taylore's Tequila Sunrise

1 ½ oz Tequila
¾ cup of orange juice
¾ cup of grenadine syrup

Major life milestones, like the death of a beloved parent, don't slow the universe down as much as we may want. As difficult as the days after my father passed were for me, I had to keep moving, although I was never the same. Things that I had previously deemed important just weren't. For this reason, unanticipated jumps were the first I was comfortable taking. When all fear was gone, and the bottom had seemingly dropped out of my life, that's when I was able to jump.

In retrospect, I should have gone to counseling after my father died. I felt a massive void in my life. Instead, I methodically went through my days with no outlet for my grief and no ability to release the pain I felt. There is a stigma attached to having mental health challenges and seeking therapy in the African American and Christian communities. Although that realization came a little too late, I now know these ideas are not healthy and believe that it's okay to have a relationship with God and see a therapist.

Time went by, and so many changes started happening so fast. Mom moved in with me and my family. Daddy wanted it that way. She needed it, and so did we. After all, we had spent so much time with Daddy and Mom over the years; it felt like it was natural and Mom, Jowell, and I comforted each other. I honestly think a huge void was felt by all of us because Daddy had such a huge personality. We transitioned from military life. Daddy always wanted me to become a teacher, so I became one. Life was especially hard for Taylore and Sterling. They didn't like the change. We were in a new environment - we were not living on a military base anymore, and they were not going to military schools. It was a culture shock for my children. Taylore and Sterling were treated differently by their peers because this was our first time living in a predominantly African American Community, and their peers picked up on that. So, Maryland was not the change Jowell and I really wanted. We only moved there so my mom would be close to my sisters, who all lived in Maryland. Looking back on it now, I realize when you are grieving, sometimes you jump for others because you are unable to make good decisions for yourself.

Nevertheless, we went about life and moved forward. The death of my father changed my whole outlook on life and the way I thought about the things I wanted for myself. But as any mother knows, you put your children's needs first. When your kids go through challenges, you have to be there for them, even when you may be an emotional wreck yourself with no outlet to channel your feelings and heal.

Honestly, though Daddy has been gone for a couple of decades, I still struggle with his loss. It's heart-wrenching to lose a parent and being able to process that grief seemed nearly impossible. There still are days when the feeling is fresh, and I feel the tears rolling down my face. My family couldn't understand why I couldn't move forward. They would say, "Daddy would want you to." As I think about it now, I am reminded of a sermon I heard by Dr. Jamal Bryant about making sure you don't allow anyone to put an expiration date on your grief. I worked hard to maintain my composure and provide some comfort to Mom, Taylore, and Jowell. Sterling was too young to remember Daddy. I could feel their pain and spent much of my time ensuring that they were all okay.

I kept busy working as a teacher and supporting the kids with their hobbies, school, and handling the dozens of decisions and activities that a mother does daily. I was grateful that my mind was occupied with these tasks and realized, only in hindsight, that the volume and normality of it all ate up so much of my time that I didn't have any time left to focus on my own thoughts and needs. At some point, I rationalized, there would be time to do that, just not "now."

Routine was a genuine savior for me. It gave me little time to sit with my thoughts. I was so busy during most of my days that I only had time to think through things at night when I was too tired to do any deep thinking. Despite being exhausted, it took me hours to fall asleep because of the difficulties I was having with my rebellious children and with myself longing for change. The rebelliousness came from them not adjusting to change themselves. I felt like I was missing something. There were times when I felt alone, and my thoughts often shifted to travel adventures past or the anticipation of future adventures.

Being a military brat and spouse, I was accustomed to being stationed all over the world. I got to visit and explore many countries, landmarks, and cultures. It was wonderful! However, I thought to myself, "Finally, I can really settle down and either start a business or work at one job consistently since we are out of the military." With so much moving, I was a late bloomer with my career. All my friends had careers right out of college. I thought I always wanted that for myself, but when it happened, I realized quickly that I didn't. I thrived better at being an entrepreneur. It was the free spirit in me and what my father instilled in our family that made me shudder at being tied down to a "nine to five." It was hard to hear friends and family complain every day about getting up and going to work. I knew I didn't want that for my life. We spend so much time with our careers, but we should always remember that we can all be replaced instantly! As drastic as this may sound, I feel when you get up and go to any place that you don't like, you make others around you miserable. I didn't want that for myself. I know some people will say, "Well, I have to do what I have to do." I understand that, but whenever you get that glimmer of hope, take the risk and allow your creator to lead you. It will be the best decision you will ever make. Going out of your comfort zone stretches you and your faith and allows you to grow into something you didn't know existed. Although Maryland wasn't hard to adjust to for me, I didn't realize how much I missed exploring new and different countries and cultures. Mostly, I was so busy being a mother that I didn't have time to think about being "me."

Things were manageable and predictable, and there were times I was grateful for this, even if it meant that the life I was living felt a little removed from what I desired. By now, Jowell had taken a contract job that moved him to the Middle East, and I instantly became a single/married person. My mom also moved out on her own, and I tried to do the same. Taylore joined The Coast Guard after high school, and before she joined Jowell and I told her that she had to learn how to tread water for at least 15 minutes since The Coast Guard's mission takes place mainly in water. I was thankful that I had a house with a pool in the backyard. Taylore was so upset and rebellious, but she learned how to do it for much longer than we asked her to. She exceeded basic training and was also in The Coast Guard Band playing the flute. Shortly after graduating from basic training, she was assigned to her first duty and was stationed near San Francisco, California.

One day while out sightseeing with one of her friends, she was in a horrific accident. She plunged 75 feet into the Pacific Ocean in a car and had to fight to save her life. She was 18 at the time. My first response was thankfulness. I was also grateful that Jowell and I made her tread water for long periods of time because that helped her to save her own life. Jowell was overseas and I had no way of contacting him. But, he and I were so connected at that moment that he said he woke up in the middle of the night, and a voice told him to call me. The accident changed Taylore's life forever. How could it not? For me, this was my second "jump." My life and the way I parented changed from that day forward.

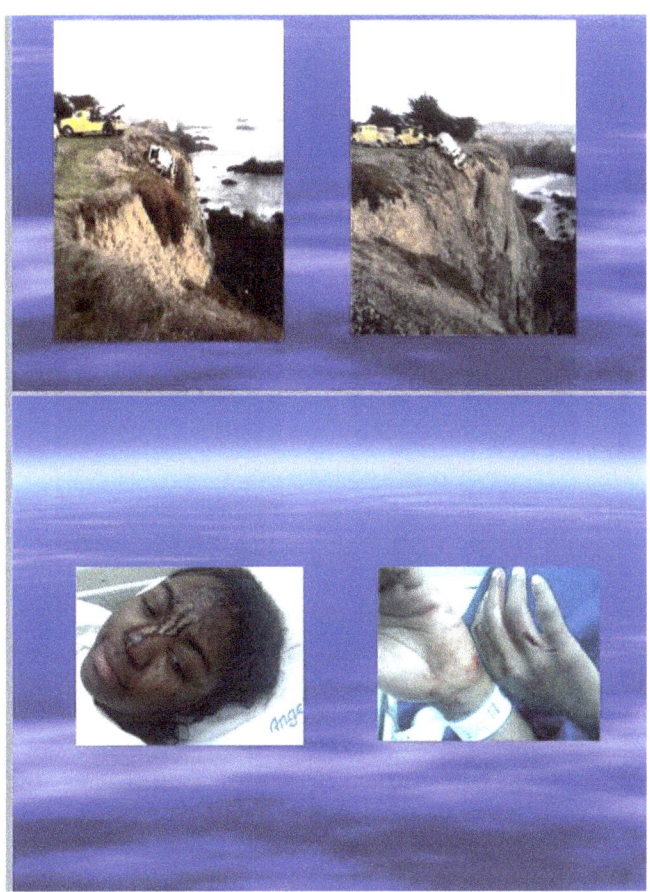

Being 18 years of age and dealing with something that horrific is hard for anyone to deal with, let alone a teenager. I promised God that I would always fight for Taylore because she had fought so hard to live. During the crash, her seat belt didn't unfasten until the car was underwater. She had to kick out the windows and swim to a rock for safety before the helicopters came to her rescue. She is the ultimate survivor, and I am so proud to be her mother! "Taylore fought to stay alive. She lived to see the next sunrise, which is why I named a special drink after her!" The Coast Guard stationed her in Annapolis, Maryland after the accident, and she was released with an Honorable Discharge later that year. Having children is a true blessing; they represent hope in our lives.

Meanwhile, Sterling was just starting high school and was a standout football player looking to attend college and hopefully play professionally one day. However, he just didn't like school. Since he was struggling, I had him tested to figure out what the mental block was for him. I remember one day he came home distraught that one of his teachers told him that he would never amount to anything because he wasn't good in school. Having a teacher say that to any child is so detrimental, and I really think that it affected him more than I knew. We transferred him to private schools, but some of the private schools' classrooms were still too large for him.

As an ex-teacher, I knew how hard it could be for some students who struggled in school to learn in an environment that was not conducive. I remember when I was a middle school teacher, I always volunteered to teach multi-level classes. Most often, children are embarrassed in front of their peers when they feel inferior in their learning. In turn, that's why most students act out in class, to hide what the real problem is. During his last two years of high school, I had to pivot and adjust my life. I homeschooled Sterling to help him regain his confidence. I was thankful for that time and it paid off because he was offered several scholarships to play football. I've always encouraged both the kids to pursue their dreams because they are so talented.

I was so devastated after Taylore's accident because the counseling didn't help. She shut me out. I tried to enroll her in bartending school after the Coast Guard to help cope with trauma. Psychologists say it's normal for teenagers who have withstood severe trauma to act out in this manner. Sterling was having mental blocks in school, and Jowell was overseas for most of it. The next year, Taylore delivered a baby that died only hours after birth. As a mother, who has never experienced either of these traumas, how do you help? I felt helpless. Children don't come with any instructions, and mothers do the best they can to deal with their struggles. Taylore became rebellious and started spiraling. She felt like the world was against her. As mothers, we are happy to drop our lives, put them on hold, and re-evaluate our whole lives for the sake of their health and well-being. Taylore and Sterling really tried moving forward despite having obstacles. I knew that I had a long road ahead of me with Taylore and Sterling, and I knew that I had to be there for them at all cost. I felt honored that God gave me the assignment.

My concern grew for my children. However, one day it hit me that they must soon both go out in the world to find their own paths. I was approaching middle age and the ordinary tasks and routines that occupied so much of my time would be gone as well. How would I occupy my time? What would I do to feel a sense of personal fulfillment? Could I still be there for them feeling unequipped to help them when they needed it the most?

In less than two years, major changes would happen. What then? Taylore and Sterling tried to live normal lives. They tried to go out and explore, but what would become of me? The discontent that I was beginning to feel day in and day out was something I ignored for weeks which turned into months. This prompted me to ask myself what would life look like for me? While I didn't know yet what I wanted to do with the rest of my life, I knew things had to change, and I knew *I* had to change especially when life threw me one more curve ball.

All marriages evolve with time. The best grow and become closer, and the worst end in bitterness, isolation, loneliness, contempt, and finally, divorce. Many people believe this is the worst thing that could happen. I didn't, and neither did Jowell. We decided as a couple that our time together was over and so we separated. Without Daddy, Jowell, Taylore, or Sterling, I had no more excuses.

Have you ever had to make a quick decision that altered the trajectory of your life?

4

READY TO JUMP

John Daly

2 oz Lemonade
2 oz Brewed Tea
1.5 oz Vodka

I was finally ready to think about my next chapter - my next
move. Being a newly separated woman left me a lot of time
to think in my empty house. Jowell was overseas, and he and I
were very good married friends. I still didn't yet know what I
wanted for myself, but I was ready for a change. A friend once
told me that a big house breeds loneliness, and I realized for the
first time that this was true. But I also knew that I now had the
opportunity to change that.

I love the water and was determined to spend the bulk of
my summer soaking up the sun and lounging by the pool within
our housing development. In addition to the pool, there was a
nearby golf club for residents to enjoy, so I had the luxury of

relaxing and enjoying lunch or cocktails there after a day in the water. Since my county at that time was in the top 10 counties for affluent African Americans, it provided the social interaction I craved in a relaxed atmosphere. It was exactly what I needed and the bonus was that it was close to home, so I could go as often as I liked.

This became my daily routine - to take my pool bag and a book out to lounge in the sun and swim. One of my favorite books is Spencer Johnson's, "Who Moved My Cheese?" It is the story of two mice, Sniff and Scurry, and two humans, Hem and Haw, whose objective is to locate cheese in a maze so that they'll have a constant supply of food. The mice learn quickly where the cheese is, and eventually the humans do as well. But the mice ultimately anticipate that the supply of cheese will dwindle and things will change, whereas the humans don't anticipate that change will happen and are less receptive and adaptable to it.

The book offers many valuable lessons, but the most important among them is to be ready to change quickly and enjoy life. This made me think and ultimately gave me hope and anticipation about the new and positive things that often come with change. It was a fun, inspirational read that reminded me to take one day at a time and just go with the flow. That summer, I spent many poolside days in my shorts, t-shirt, and flip-flops (my favorite shoes), enjoying the scenery and conversations with friends. After hours at the pool, I'd head to the clubhouse for a drink or two to relax and socialize. It was paradise! Eventually, the weight of my unhappiness lifted and vanished in the summer heat. Those were perfect summer days, and I felt fortunate to enjoy such a good life. I just enjoyed my summer routine and tried not to stress when confronting the significant life changes that were rapidly approaching.

One afternoon, I stopped by the clubhouse for a quick drink. Recognizing the manager, who I'd made friends with, I shouted a quick "Hey, John" and walked to my regular table outside with the drink that I'd just ordered at the bar. John came by.

"It looks like you are slammed today," I told him.

"Yeah, we are shorthanded today and the bar is crowded and we only have one bartender." I scanned the area near the bar and saw people lined up waiting impatiently to place their drink orders.

"I'm not busy right now. I can help out for a while if you want," I offered.

"Sure, I could use a hand, and I know you make a mean drink," he said. I explained to him that I could because I had just finished going to bartending school. I've always believed in making sure I was well trained when I tried new things.

I got up from my regular table and made my way through the crowd to go to the bathroom and wash my hands. When I was done, I met John at the bar, and for the remainder of the evening, took drink orders and made each drink carefully as John handled the register. I worked hard to keep up with the bustling Thursday night crowd. Because I loved people, I had a great time making cocktails, saying hello to familiar faces, and meeting new patrons as we served everyone as quickly as we could.

When the night was over, John thanked me for pitching in and offered me a job as a bartender at the club. At first, I thought he was joking, but he mentioned that he had a hard time finding good bartenders and that I'd done a fantastic job just pitching in for the night. He made his appeal and said I'd make great money. And because he knew me, he added that I would still get to enjoy camaraderie with old friends and meet new people while having fun. He thought I was perfect for the job. I realized as he was talking that I did have a fantastic time pitching in. It probably would be a fun job for the summer and the excitement I felt at the opportunity let me know that this was just the jump I needed - the jump into a brand new career as a bartender. So why not? I said yes, and the Sunset Bartender was born! I was now grateful that after the Coast Guard, when I tried to enroll Taylore in bartending school, that she didn't go and I did. I was elated that I did not let that opportunity go to waste.

The Sunset Bartender is Born

It was just a couple of nights a week at first, the busy nights, and then it became a regular gig - something I looked forward to and was good at. Thursday night became "Cigar Night." It took off, and I even secured a local car dealership to sponsor the event. Customers enjoyed hand-rolled cigars and live music. After a few weeks of bartending at the clubhouse and building up an easy rapport with new customers and friends, the patrons would ask for me and wanted to know when I'd be working so they could stop by, say hello and enjoy a few cocktails while I was there. I was flattered and thrilled that they thought highly of my skills as a bartender. My customers said I was a great listener and easy to talk to. The job was set around a lake at the ninth hole. I knew from the start that most patrons who came to the bar were looking for relaxation, an escape, and often a listening ear, especially one attached to a friendly face that they recognized. People will tell their bartender things that they won't admit to their mate or closest confidante. They're looking for confirmation, an opinion without judgment, and sometimes, just someone who will listen to them. Visiting their local clubhouse surrounded by friends and neighbors offered that gratification and a good time. Just like John Daly, the golfer for whom this chapter's drink is named, did for the people around him, I brightened people's day with my conversation and a smile!

As a bartender, I met people of all races with backgrounds as different as the sunsets, and it has taught me that people across all cultures have more in common than they can ever imagine. When I poured someone a beer or created a craft cocktail with their favorite spirit of choice, I got to talk with the most interesting, beautiful people and they were always happy to see me and eager to have a listening ear. This relationship was reciprocal – I learned from them, and they inspired me. Bartending was a way to not only engage in a social pleasantry and also lift your spirits (pun intended), provided that it is not abused.

My customers knew me so well that one of them, Dean, gave me the name, "The Sunset Bartender." He noticed every day while I was working, I would stop what I was doing to take a picture of the sunset. The colors of a sunset give me so much joy. Have you ever really looked at one from the onset until it fades? It is moving and changing every second and transforming by the minute. Furthermore, depending on where you capture the sunset, the experience changes. For example, I prefer sunsets over the ocean. Ocean sunsets seem endless and offer, to the eyes, endless possibilities.

Thursday nights at Lake Presidential Club House turned into a huge night every week. I met the most wonderful people bartending at the clubhouse, and hospitality came easy for me. I was groomed for it at an early age by my parents. I was so thankful for groups like the Virginia State University (VSU) Alumni Association and my college friends who supported me. Kim Whitlock and Terry Parker were very pivotal in making sure VSU stayed connected in The Washington DC/VA/MD area (DMV). One thing about VSU is that we are a family and always show love and support for one another. I also have tremendous gratitude for Erica Zentz, who rallied for Cigar Nights. After all, it was a country club, but it transformed into the social event of the week on Thursday nights. Erica saw the genius of it and the profit it generated. I also want to thank Jay Walker, who also played a major role in introducing me to a large group of people who became family.

While I was working in the club one day, a gentleman attending a golf outing gave me his business card and said he would hire me on the spot if I ever wanted to work for him at a hotel at The National Harbor in Maryland. He just happened to be the Director of Operations and I took him up on that offer and went to work there for several months. At the National Harbor, the events grew bigger. Although it was fun to entertain my customers, I was still unfulfilled. I worked there until the hotel was sold and was very blessed that my old job in my community allowed me to return. Still, something felt off. I couldn't quite put my finger on it, but I was starting to get the nagging feeling that I needed to make a significant change in order to experience new energy. I needed to jump!

Developing the Mindset to Jump

One evening, after a long day at work, I came home exhausted. To pass the time, I logged into my social media account and saw a video posted on my timeline of one of the Kings of Comedy, Steve Harvey, who was now the host of the game show "Family Feud." The YouTube clip was a video of Steve's conversation with the studio audience before taping the show about living your purpose. "I'm going to tell you something. I'm going to share something that every successful person has to do, including you. Believe it or not, every successful person in this world has jumped. I'm going to tell you what I mean by that," he said. "You cannot just exist in this life. You have to try to live. If you are waking up thinking that there's got to be more to your life than there is – man, believe that there is. Believe in your heart of hearts that it is. But to get to that life, you're going to have to jump."

Steve went on to explain that God endows everyone with unique talents that they should leverage in building a life of purpose and happiness. "Everyone has a gift, and you must identify that gift. The Bible says your gift will make room for you. If you're just getting up every day and going to a job that you hate working, that ain't living – that's existing." Steve explained that the only way to see what living is like is to jump.

"When you first try to jump," he said, "your parachute will not open right away. You're going to hit rocks. You're going to get some cuts, but eventually, the parachute has to open. You can play it safe, and deal with the cuts and the tears, or you can stand on that cliff of life forever safe. But if you don't jump, your parachute will never open. You'll never know what God really has for you." That message hit me hard, and I literally thought he was speaking directly to me. I don't believe in coincidence. I knew it was time to jump.

Sterling was now living in California. He didn't do well at his first school academically. He was still on a quest to play football and follow his dream, and schools were still pursuing him. He was struggling and making poor choices because he loved the game, but education was both the pathway to his dream and his roadblock. The urge within me wanted to be there for him. He was over 18 at this point, but as parents, you still must guide your children and allow them to make their own choices at the same time. Coaches would promise him things, however at this point, I think the ball was dropped from both ends. As mothers, we always want to be with our children (no matter how grown they are) when we see them struggling or hurting. I knew I needed the change and would open tremendous possibilities for me, even if my motivation was to help my son.

God knew how to take me out of my comfort zone, and he knew that only Taylore or Sterling could do it. As I said, Sterling's ultimate dream of playing at a higher level had been dashed. He knew that he had talents, but there was no way to do it without education, and he was devastated. He hit a wall, so I knew then that I had to "Double Dutch" jump for him *and myself.*

Anyone who has ever confronted the prospect of rebuilding a life can tell you that there's a lot of uncertainty involved. Change is hard at first, messy in the middle, and gorgeous at the end. Yet, even though it would be hard, I had no stress. Nothing motivates a mom like a hurting child. I felt calmer and more centered than I had in a long time once I finally decided to jump. As I thought about all of the transitions that were about to happen in my life, I thought about butterflies and how they morph at different stages during their development.

I have always loved butterflies! They are colorful, fanciful, and free, and deep down, I always thought I had a lot in common with them. I have always felt the freedom to be myself and be comfortable in my skin. That feeling was heightened now. Something about making major life decisions lifted a weight that I'd unconsciously been carrying. I felt the anticipation and excitement that comes with the thought of new possibilities. I also felt blessed by God with endless mercies, and that feeling was with me daily.

I knew, of course, that I would have to find work. One great benefit of being a bartender is that you can do it anywhere. Despite the necessity of work, I also knew that having time to relax and just go with the flow as I figured out the following chapters of my life was also important. I felt unrushed, and I knew that somehow, a more complete plan would begin to unfold if I just trusted God.

Sterling is a jumper also, but he was jumping for football. He refused to return to Maryland because he believed his failure had begun there. I didn't understand why he felt that way when I'd always been there to support him and lift his spirits. I knew at my core that he needed me, even if he couldn't ask me to come. At the same time, Taylore had a good life even though it wasn't always steady, so I knew that she was maintaining.

How could I be in two places? They both needed me. Jowell was back and had started another job. I needed to help Sterling since he was three thousand miles away. I decided that this is how I would make my jump. I told my co-worker, Deanna, the real reason I was moving to California. I didn't want to share my plans with anyone, in part because I'd made up my mind and didn't want anyone to persuade me otherwise. You have to give yourself time and space alone to make big decisions.

I was already questioning myself enough because I had never been on my own. I left for college, got married, and then moved wherever the Army took us. I didn't know if I was physically prepared to be alone. I only knew that I was a mother and I was needed. I asked Jowell to go and help me, but he had just started a new career in the government and couldn't. I then solicited the help of a friend who was the only person other than Jowell who knew the depth of my struggles with Taylore and Sterling. He had known them since they were small. Fortunately, he agreed to come along for the jump.

Having made the decision to go, I was filled with emotions, anticipation, excitement, and also concern. How do you prepare for the unknown? I felt that the jump was right, but what was I jumping to? I knew, even though I desperately wanted to change, I'd have a lot of decisions to make. I felt a bit overwhelmed because there was so much to do and to consider. Although I was determined to go help my son and to change my own path in the process, I was also fearful after I decided to jump.

Jumps are filled with faith, fear, and hope, but also as Steve Harvey said, rocks. You can't see in advance all the things you may not be prepared for, and sometimes, you can't know what you will experience beforehand. Despite all of that, I knew I'd made the right decision. I also knew that I'd have to find a job. A huge part of California's economy is its tourism industry. I rationalized that finding work as a bartender would be easy in California. I had interviews scheduled in anticipation of my arrival, and things were progressing along just fine in my preparation to jump.

Remember the first time you drove to the ocean? Not the beach, but the ocean. A big, beautiful, vast body of water that is endless and lapping with waves. You may have been driving to it with anticipation – looking forward to reaching it and when you finally, finally get there, you just wanted to be a part of it, even as you realize that it could swallow you up and leave you bruised and battered. It's exhilarating! That's what a jump feels like. You see the waves, but also the uncertainty and the risk. Jumps come with a lot of tears, beauty and freedom, but most importantly with endless possibilities. The waves? Those are the rough times. I also landed on some rocks. But each time I jumped, I viewed it as an opportunity to learn and grow.

I've always been the type of person that shares things with people. I've always felt that you can come back from anything, which I used to motivate and fuel myself as well as my children. I didn't feel embarrassed or ashamed to admit that I didn't have all the answers, and in some respects, things were failing in my life at the time. I didn't pretend that everything was perfect. In fact, I told people that things weren't perfect. Yet, I was jumping anyway. I made it public to my friends and family and on my social media that the countdown had started to my big jump, but I didn't provide details. Despite having more questions than answers, I felt confident that things would align for me.

To jump, you have to have FAITH that God will supply your needs and be with you every step of the way. Once you get to know how FAITH works, then you must understand favor. I was thankful for both, and little did I know how much I was going to need them as time progressed. One thing I know is that if God brings you to anything in your life, He will bring you through it. When you believe in God and operate in FAITH, some things may take you out of your comfort zone, but God is still in control. I have gone through some tough things that led me to grow, particularly when I made mistakes. If I hadn't made the decisions I had, I wouldn't have grown as much as I did. Those personal failures in life ultimately make you better.

When I decided to leave what some deemed a good life – a nice home, a nice car, literally being a kept woman – I knew that anyone I told would think I was crazy. But that's exactly what I'd decided to do. I had a plan and it was simple: I'd sell everything and get rid of all of the stuff that I'd accumulated over the years. I had beautiful things – furniture, clothing, jewelry and purses that meant so much to me at one time. Getting rid of those things, though, gave me even more joy because I knew that selling them would give me the money I needed to fund my cross-country jump, something that I was more determined than ever to do.

In about one month's time, I'd made the arrangements that I needed to make, sold my belongings and began to pack the things I'd take with me. All the things that had meaning to me and that I needed were packed, and just like that, I'd reduced 51 years of living and 28 years of marriage into the trunk of my car, which I shipped to California. It was Mother's Day and traditionally, my job was hosting Mother's Day Brunch, so my mother and sisters came out to support me and say their goodbyes. It was hard for my mother to see me leave. I asked Jowell to please watch over Taylore and let me go to Sterling since he couldn't come to California. And with that one final act, my big jump began.

5

Navigating in Flight

Sterling's Sidecar

2 oz cognac
1 oz Cointreau
1 oz fresh lemon juice
Lime for Garnish
Superfine sugar rim

California's beaches, weather, and natural beauty draw people from all over the world, and its hospitality industry is legendary. Armed with my previous experiences, I was equipped to enter as the newest member of the California workforce and felt well-prepared by my father to serve drinks and give exceptional hospitality. I had a company that was interested in me working for them. My first interview went well, and I was prepared for the second one to seal the deal as planned and become the newest bartender at a new property. I was enthusiastic and couldn't wait for the second interview. As soon as I arrived, I received a message that there would be a delay in the opening. I wish things went as smoothly in real life as I had imagined they would in my head.

I was devastated. I'd moved with the expectation that I'd have a job quickly which would allow me to find an apartment that I could afford and get settled. Now, the job that I'd expected fell through, and I'd have to hustle to get another one. It was a major blow that sent me into a bit of a panic. I hit the ground running! Compounding the rush to get a job was the insane housing market in California in 2016. The rental market in San Diego was very competitive, and available apartments were at a premium. I'd made hotel reservations for the first couple of weeks in the city, but because of the influx of meetings and conventions occurring, my crew and I had to hotel hop for weeks. Thankfully, I readjusted quickly. Being a military kid and spouse helps with that.

Getting a job was my number one priority. That was my first blow, and I questioned my decision to jump more than once. Yet, there was a voice deep inside me that told me to remain faithful, stay the course, and believe that eventually, everything would work out for the best.

One day while out driving to the beach, I came across a billboard across the street at the hotel where I was staying which said, "Bartenders Wanted." Remember, I don't believe in coincidence. I walked in and literally walked out with the job – which was a blessing.

I could have folded when I learned that the job I'd planned wasn't going to materialize, but my FAITH kicked in, and God showed up to give me the sign that I'd been looking for. I knew that I was taking the right steps. I was so glad that I had ridden in "Sterling's Sidecar" to California! A huge bonus for me was that my new manager was from Germany, and I knew a lot about the country, having lived there when I was first married. This immediately established a bond between us. About 10 days after I landed the job, Taylore decided to join us in California and immediately found a job as well. She really could have been independent out there, if the housing market was different. She is so smart and resourceful. So, my entire family was now on the West Coast. The only difference was that we didn't have a home anymore like we did in Maryland.

When I moved to the state of California, legislation on medical cannabis had just passed and Sterling explained to me how, if used correctly, it could help all of us since it is prescribed by doctors for a variety of ailments including vertigo, which I suffer from and have been previously hospitalized for. Taylore was looking for natural remedies because she didn't want to take medicine for her trauma. After Sterling told me about it, I took a class to learn more. Honestly, I didn't know the depths of it.

But what I did know was how my family felt about it. Taking that class is considered a leap, which is an example of doing things that aren't on your path. I was looking for solutions to help my children heal.

I learned about the uses of medical cannabis and how it aided in people who suffered from trauma. I hired a lawyer and decided to change the narrative about what I was taught. I secured an office space and proceeded in opening up my own version of a dispensary. I turned it into a place of healing. I adorned it with salt lamps, diffusers and healing music, and offered a place for people to come in to heal. I also used my hospitality skills to make people feel safe. At the time, Maryland hadn't passed any legislation, so what I was doing took on a different connotation for my family. Sometimes you have to unlearn what you've been taught. Although I could see that it would have been profitable, I closed it down immediately because of my family values. I look back now and see how the world has changed along with people's views. I am so thankful to Taylore and Sterling for opening my eyes to change, even if the world didn't agree. Fast forward to today, African Americans who own dispensaries are few. What a blessing that would have been to people who suffer from chronic ailments and diseases; to have people who really care about their well being and having ownership in that. Oh well, you move forward in faith; I learned so much from that experience and I am a better person because of it.

My early days in San Diego were filled with tending bar and interacting with some of the most beautiful people. I have the spirit of a hostess and servant, so it was easy for me to meet and connect with diverse people as a bartender in a high-end hotel. The people I met were warm, open, and chatty, and they were from all over the globe, especially Europe. San Diego, California is known for perfect weather almost year-round. Most people I met were in the city on vacation and were very generous with gratuities and even gifts for what they said was "incredible" service. I started receiving 5-star reviews with customers from all around the world. It was on a different level because they weren't people I knew.

I worked a lot of hours to build up a customer base. I think the secret weapon that prepared me for this role was my Daddy teaching me about hospitality, which after all, is what California tourism is all about. I was great at my job and loved what I was doing and my jump had landed me in a beautiful state where I gained a renewed sense of self and could assist my children. I'm so honored that God gave me the strength and the courage to act upon my instinct to jump. Because jumps are sometimes for others – they can be a way to show them that the impossible can be done and it gives others the courage and permission to do the same.

We hotel hopped for months since we hadn't yet found a place to live. My saving grace was I was staying on military bases. Taylore, Sterling, and I were back where we felt safe. We felt at home. I was a traveling bartender and making money every day. The people at all the military bases knew of me and my family. On my days off, I would cook for the hotel staff. Base maintenance workers, housekeepers, and even front desk staff frequented my room. They'd smell my cooking and stop by. We became a family. They even brought their families to meet me and would go grocery shopping to ask if I needed anything to add to what I was already cooking. I didn't understand that type of openness and welcoming at first, but it was so refreshing. I was living a new dream and it was exciting. Home is literally where your heart is!

San Diego has at least six military bases. Coronado Island, which is home to million-dollar homes, was one of my favorites. It boasts resort living with a full kitchen, den, and bedroom in every suite. It was everything I needed – and all for under $70. Most of the hotel staff looked forward to me being off work. We would go to the beach, have bonfires, sit, and talk endlessly as we watched the ocean waves. Being a bartender and a friendly person made our conversations easy. They felt at ease, and so did I.

Although we lived room-to-room in San Diego, I enjoyed it! I know I shouldn't have, but I loved every minute of my time there, and I developed a love for resort living. I thought maybe I'd been a little hasty in jumping to San Diego completely without a safety net or cheering squad (although my family supported me from afar.) People sometimes believe that faith rids you of fear, but that isn't always true. You can have incredible faith and still be a little afraid at times. It's just that eventually, your faith drives out all that fear and that's where you truly find yourself. I'm sure by now you are thinking I never want to jump. As I mentioned before, jumping is not for everyone. It's easy to throw in the towel or walk away from failures. It takes courage and faith to remain. My motto is, "You have to decide what kind of life you really want, and then say NO to everything that isn't that." That's exactly what I did.

The lifestyle I wanted was the beautiful views, nice weather, beautiful flowers, flip flops year-round, sunsets and above all, the ocean. I knew those things brought me peace. As we let our guards down, we sometimes get complacent and pick up old habits instead of developing new ones. Jumps allow them to fall off again, which in turn increases our faith. It makes it a lot easier for pivots or sudden changes that are preventable. In turn, faith becomes your reality for everything you do. When you land from jumping, all you need is your feet planted on the ground.

When I decided to jump, I was leaving family and friends, some of whom I'd known for years as well as some new ones. I also documented my journey and shared it on my social media channels. I had developed a nice following of people who would message me and tell me that I was an inspiration to them. I knew even as they told me this that many of the people who followed me may have also wanted a change. They may have wanted to make a jump of their own, but didn't know how and were afraid. I subconsciously began to make mental notes of my thoughts and fears as I made moves that took me out of my comfort zone, and knew that they would be helpful to other people who would need motivation to change their own lives with a jump. More often than not, when you fail at things, you are never taken backward. Failing propels you forward, because it allows you to see the mistakes and aids you in making better decisions in the future. It was then that I decided to write about how and why to jump.

The beauty of my jump is that I knew I always had a place to go back to, and that gave me

Keith Copeland is 😊 feeling positive. ⋯
May 9, 2016 · 👥

Somebody is going to have to step up there game and fill a huge void....my boo is about to Jump. I can't believe Freetobeme is about to leave from being a short drive away. Sunsets will always be a favorite time of day to reflect on my bartender. My attitude is good, yours is better.

a sense of security that I was thankful for. My family would have embraced my return, and I was humbled by the freedom that gave me. I knew that in changing my life, I'd have to rely on God. It felt good to literally live out God's word, like in Matthew 6:26, "Look at the birds of the air, they do not sow or reap, store away barns and yet your heavenly Father feeds them. Are you more valuable than them?" God's word came true in my life with each jump, and it was in those moments that I knew that God had me in the palm of his hand.

I knew that I was going to be on a whirlwind, and I braced myself for what was to come. I needed to break away from my past and had to be stripped down and built back up again. I couldn't believe all the messages I got from people who were following my journey and felt inspired. But, I also heard rumors about some of the people I used to serve who were speaking negatively about me. Either way, I was fueled. I was energized daily and more importantly, I knew I was loved. As the Bible says in Romans 8:31(KJV), "If God be for us, who can be against us?"

I remember one post that I put on Facebook that was particularly relevant to the situations that I encountered. It read, "I've slept in beds, on couches, floors, the beach, and in cars, but God never slept on me." It was a struggle. I became a tourist while living in California. I became adventurous and did things that I've never done. It was wonderful to experience the city this way, but things were far from perfect. Things were just not falling into place as I expected. As a matter of fact, it was the opposite. I was still excited but also anxious. I never questioned my creator nor my FAITH. I experienced it first hand on this journey. I kept moving forward. I went to bed every night in peace, knowing that God is bigger than anything I will face tomorrow. As you are skipping, leaping, and jumping, you begin to realize that you are just not the same person.

Even though things weren't perfect by a long shot, I felt alive. I felt like I had a purpose. I was putting God's word to the test, which is what we must do if we are expecting big moves of faith. I literally was living one day at a time on purpose. One thing you must know if you're thinking about jumping, is that sometimes you will get a little sore from the constant friction of it. But I knew I needed to do it. My soul felt alive.

Although I had incredible faith that God would provide for me, that didn't mean I was completely without fear. Fear can be a paralyzing emotion if you let it. Somewhere deep inside, that unsettled feeling crept in all too frequently, and it was constant work to get it to subside. I knew that my life would be so much better if I could break free of the fear that I felt, so I worked hard to overcome it. That often required me to do some reflecting on my past experiences. In the words of Robert Ludlum, "Hope is the ONLY thing stronger than fear."

When I was a sixth-grade teacher doing continuing education classes in Washington D.C., I was assigned to read "The Fourth Little Pig" by Teresa Celsi and complete a paper about it. In this book, the story picks up where "The Three Little Pigs" left off. The three pigs are now living in a brick house together. They are too afraid to come out, because they are still scared of the wolf. The sister, who is the fourth pig, comes to the house to find that all the pigs haven't left the house because of their fear that the wolf will return. She tells her brothers that "there is so much to do and see outside." That story stuck with me because I could relate. I was doing the same thing day in and day out. It was boring. I was just existing. I knew there was so much more to life. Why would God create this big world and not want us to explore it? The fourth pig offers hope. However, I also believe there's another important lesson to the story: sometimes we allow fear to keep us from living up to our true potential. But in the words of Zach Williams, "Fear is a liar."

All my life, I'd been sheltered and protected. I'd been protected by my parents, especially my father, who would tell my older sisters not to mess with "That Baby." When I left home for college at 18 and eventually married my husband four years later, I was thrust from one protective bubble to another.

I spent years as a military brat and wife and traveled much of the world. I gained many new perspectives on different cultures and enjoyed different experiences, but I had still been sheltered. Because of that, I realized for the first time that I had an overwhelming sense of fear when it came to being truly independent, without being subject to anyone else's thoughts or demands for my life.

The realization that I was afraid hit me hard because I'd never thought of myself as a fearful person. I wasn't sure that I knew how to move from a place where I was surrounded by the fear of what came next. I knew, however, that I'd have to jump to it for my next phase. So, I did.

I moved to Orange County and lived in Westminster, California, which is known for its many Vietnamese refugees who migrated in 1980. It was a new experience, and I enjoyed experiencing the new cultures. My friend, Adreena Martin, who I met when I lived in Germany, helped me get a job working at The Hyatt Regency close to Disneyland. I exceeded expectations there as well but developed pneumonia shortly thereafter. God showed me that my illness "was not unto death." He told me that He needed that time to prepare me for what was to come. He used those seven days to minister to me and told me He was pleased with my faith. The enemy must ask God's permission for the attacks. I did not waver in my faith and thus, He would see me through.

I was in ICU for a week and was unable to go back to work because it took a little longer to heal. Every time I was faced with difficulty, I would always see the numbers 11:11. It appeared on my phone, clocks, and billboards. I didn't understand it. It was happening frequently. I researched its meaning and saw that I wasn't alone. According to www.biblestudy.org, the meaning represents joyful praise and gratitude of God's mercy and love. I was reminded of the scripture 1 Corinthians 1:27 (AMP), "But God has selected [for His purpose] the foolish things of the world to shame the wise [revealing their ignorance]." I had to remind myself again of what inspired me to jump in the first place. I thought of the song entitled, "When You Think About Quitting, Remember Why You Started," by Fearless Motion. I can't explain why I didn't throw in the towel and just go back home, but God knew that I needed confirmation to keep going, and He provided that time and again. I knew I could go back at any time but, for whatever reason, I had no desire to go back. For me, in the words of Donna Karan, it was all about finding "calm in the chaos."

I'm not going to lie, I felt like whoever said you can't hit a moving target is the biggest liar in the world. I had moved across the country, faced the uncertainty of not having a job, the constant search for an apartment, and now pneumonia. Expecting the next shoe to drop didn't make it any easier. But then, I remembered the words of Dave Willis. He said, "Pray when you feel like worrying. Give thanks when you feel like complaining. Keep going when you feel like quitting."

Shortly after I got out of the hospital with pneumonia, I came home one day to divorce papers, because Jowell and I were still only separated and not divorced yet. My body was still weak and recovering, and now my heart was faced with the new trauma of ending a marriage to the man who had been my best friend for decades. It was so much to bear at one time. Although he and I talked almost every day and we knew we had to end our marriage legally, it was still heartbreaking.

I prayed to God to show me a way to get through to the other side of all of it. I prayed that He would show me how to release the life I had in order to embrace the new life that was waiting for me. I said, "Lord, I'm thankful for this day. Give me the strength to face everything that is before me, embrace freedom, find belonging and still myself so that I can be an inspiration to other people. Teach me how to live intentionally and fearlessly while leaving a positive footprint in the world. Guide me, in Jesus' name."

I felt like I was in a downward spiral. Nothing about my journey was going as expected, but God never changed and never failed to reveal himself as a fixture in my life. I will always be indebted to my customers and friends, J. B. and Nichel Braithaite, for helping me monetarily at the last minute to hire a lawyer in Maryland. I was still recovering from pneumonia and wasn't working at the time. They are examples of what I mentioned earlier: when customers became family. That one act allowed me to handle my business and get back on my feet, and for that, I will always be forever grateful to them. I absolutely love them, and I am confident that God used them to help me!

One of my favorite movies is The Lion King. Simba thought he was the reason his father was killed. His uncle, who wanted to be King, told him to "run and never come back." That's exactly how Jowell made me feel when he told me something similar. He said I should never return to Maryland. I didn't understand why he would say something like that to me. In the movie, Simba ran away because he was hurt and scared. What his Uncle told him made him afraid of how people would think about him. Simba met some unusual people that maybe he shouldn't have been with. He was not living up to his calling and was just existing with guilt and shame. Well, that's almost how I felt. I thought, "How could someone judge me in that manner without hearing my side?" Simba and his unusual pack became family. He grew, but his growth was different. When you go through so many changes, your mindset changes with it. You allow old ways to fall off. You adapt and pivot, your mind opens to things that you necessarily wouldn't do. That's what skips, leaps, and jumps are all about. You change and adapt when different occurrences happen in your life. Simba's new acquaintances accepted him the way he was. Sometimes, that's a great thing because when you are around the same people, they will not allow you to grow because they are comfortable with the way things are. They like to remind you of the things you used to do instead of allowing you to move forward.

I started meeting people who didn't look like me. Nor did they have the same experiences as I did. But, I was so excited to be around them. I'd found "my tribe." They were sun-gazers, giggers, free spirits, and beach lovers. I call us "The Misfits." We don't fit into molds, but we are needed to help balance the world. I remember my mom saying to me, "You and your friends can do the same thing, but you will always be the one who gets caught." I didn't understand it at the time, but boy, was she right. I've always lived out loud, and some of my friends' parents didn't care for me. I knew it even as a young adult, and it didn't bother me because I knew that I was doing exactly what their children were doing. I just lived out loud. I always had this motto that my dad used, "Live and allow others to live," and I hold true to that today. I don't know why we judge others so harshly.

The newness of what I was experiencing was unlike any feeling I've ever felt. I felt alive and free. I was on a journey to freedom. These people were some of the most adventures and positive people I've met. It was a breath of fresh air. I never worried about how I would be able to pay for living arrangements or how I would help Sterling, who had enrolled into another college (because colleges kept pursuing him). I knew I'd make it work. Hours were long, but the weather was beautiful. Every night, I would drive to the ocean and just watch the waves roll in or walk on the beach and smell the fresh air. I felt a sense of peace and stillness that I never felt anywhere else. I'd walk on the beach and sometimes record videos to share with my family and friends back East. The ocean renewed me and gave me hope daily.

I had good days – days when the weather was great, and I had pleasant customers who were good tippers and great conversationalists. But I also had a few tough days – days when my body was tired from the long hours. The people I loved most, my mother and sisters, sometimes disagreed with my decisions, and I hated to disappoint them. But, I also knew that living the life I wanted would be a priority for me. The freedom and agency to make exactly the decisions I wanted was a powerful motivator. I still felt grateful that I'd made the jump. I felt that California was just what I needed, and it was a kind of balm to soothe my soul.

With faith, I moved forward fearlessly and with a sense of freedom that was cathartic. I admit that at the time I felt like a failure in some sense because my marriage would soon be ending. But I knew that was for the best, so I forgave myself for it. I felt like every obstacle that I faced and every situation I experienced was meant to teach me to be dependent on God and to have the faith to move forward confidently with my decisions. Every obstacle and every defeat that I managed to overcome was designed to show me how strong I was, and I received my lesson. Although my victories seem small, nevertheless, they were victories and I grew from them. Every setback was a beautiful struggle and lesson about depending on God.

6

Jumping in Silence

Blue Hawaii

¾ oz vodka
¾ oz light rum
½ oz blue curacao
3 oz pineapple juice
1 oz sweet and sour mix
pineapple wedge and umbrella

After I left Orange County, I made a huge jump to Hawaii. Sterling had yet another school that pursued him and was giving him scholarships. My heart ached for him. It had to be hard to know you're sought after and offered free education to play the game you love and have it halted time after time. I wanted it to end, but I didn't want to be a dream killer. I spent so much money on tutors.

I was offered the job over the phone by the same man I worked for at The National Harbor in Maryland. He was now a

Director of Operations at The Hyatt in Honolulu. I knew that I needed isolation. Sometimes God calls you to be alone. Living in Hawaii with your friends and family on the East Coast, it is very hard to communicate because of the time difference. I only kept in contact with a few people daily besides family. I needed to hear God's voice without interruptions, and I needed to prepare my mind for legally ending my marriage. The date of my divorce was approaching, and I needed to hear nothing but God. I was working in what some people call paradise, and I realized then that those who put their faith in God's hands are covered.

One of my first experiences in Hawaii came from a supervisor. He took me to the side after being there for two days to give me advice on working and living in Hawaii. He was from South Africa. He said, "Remember who you are and remember why you were chosen to work here." It felt like the scene from The Lion King – the part when Rafiki got a sign that Simba was alive. Everyone thought Simba had died. Simba felt like a failure because he knew his father died saving him, very much like our Father in Heaven who died for all of us. When Rafiki found Simba, he had to remind him who he was. He told him that he could either run from past hurts or learn from them. Some of the people who I used to talk to daily hadn't heard from me. I had shut everyone off. I felt that in solitude, I could find myself.

My supervisor said, "I don't know why I'm telling you this, but you have to know why you were chosen to work in Hawaii." He further said, "Do you know how hard it is to get a job here?" I sat in awe and silence and took in everything. I felt so blessed, especially because I didn't have to interview for the job. I literally was chosen because of my skill set. It was like he was giving me a crash course. I thought about a sermon I heard from Bishop Noel Jones, when he said that God will break the rules to bless you. I thought about knowing how the job was offered to me and the words my supervisor said to me. He told me of the traditions and spiritual beliefs of the island and explained how to show respect to the island and its culture. My Hawaii experience was the closest I had felt to Maryland, because it was filled with family values and my customers were similar to my customers back home.

"People come from all around the world to visit what some deem as paradise. You are working here in the capacity to help make paradise even greater." I was in utter disbelief and humbled to be chosen for such a huge task. How does one make coming on vacation to paradise even better? After receiving gifts and 5-star reviews, I was so thankful to God for the opportunity. Guests would literally come to the bar and sit my whole shift and allow me to serve them. I learned about so many things from people during this time. Language barriers did not affect my great customer service or hospitality. I am still friends with some of the people I met in Hawaii. My supervisor went on to say that I needed to "Take in the Aloha." As you know, Hawaii is "The Aloha State." The meaning of Hawaii is love and friendship. He further said, "It is all about giving and receiving." Our creator gives us beautiful weather and the traditions of a people who are grounded in faith. What you have to give is authenticity, love, forgiveness, and grace, and your reward will come daily as the water ebbs and flows. 'A 'ohe Hana nui ke alu 'ia is another wonderful saying, which means "No task is too big when it's done together."

That is exactly what I learned through this whole experience. The people that live on the island are one big family. What a beautiful God-given experience! It was so powerful that it changed me. I would never be the same again. In Hawaii, I met a woman that my friend Keith introduced me to by way of his fraternity brother. She took me in and made me family instantly. I know she was God-sent. Faith always disagrees with evidence.

Although I didn't stay in Hawaii for long, being there gave me a crash course in taking my power back, and I will cherish that forever. God poured so heavily into me so fast. I didn't know why until I got a message from Sterling one day with a picture of how far I was away from him. Sterling and I would share text messages and I guess at one point, he realized that

Hawaii was a long way from where he was, and he just missed me. Until then, I'd never truly felt the distance because we could always talk by looking at a map where he had pinned my location. I literally was in the middle of the Pacific Ocean. I was too far away. Paradise was the perfect place to get renewed and to feel God's love. Hawaii is simply beautiful! I knew from that one text, I would have to jump again.

The "Hawaii Jump" was power-packed with God's outpouring of love, empowerment, and grace. I knew that jump was just for me only. It represented so much of what the next phase of my life was becoming. The people I encountered while working in Hawaii were all inspirations. I don't think I've ever met a group of people like that in my life. People who traveled from far away to work there. I was honored for that experience and fueled by the outpouring of private messages. I was living a life full of adventure and that was what my soul was crying for. I didn't miss the house, and I couldn't care less about name brands. I felt like I had more. It was fulfilling. Hawaii is the place where I spent the least amount of time, but it filled me with the most knowledge and a spiritual awakening unlike any experience that I've ever had while working. Again, I received inspirational messages from friends who felt inspired by my jumps and wanted to encourage me to keep living out loud.

Stacy Fitzgerald-Redd
May 9, 2016 · Springfield, VA · 🖾

It is an ordinary Monday, but I am encouraged and happy about people who do extraordinary things on ordinary days. Today, someone I admire had the courage to uproot her life and leave the comfortable and the familiar to follow her heart. That takes guts. I admire her fortitude. That is strength. #GetChuSome! Nothing but blessings coming your way, Freetobeme L'Tanya

Hi L'Tanya! I hope you're doing well with everything going on , i was thinking about you a while ago watching a series set in Hawaii and I just wanted to say how inspirational you are to just jump and go! I wish i could be as fearless as you! I really hope all is all!

JUN 04, 2020, 5:37 PM

You literally just made me cry! I'm so thankful and humbled! Life is so short! We have to ensure that we are living and loving our life!
You're a beautiful Queen!
I am well, I pray that you are as well!

7

LEAPING BACK TO CALI

Los Angeles Classic Martini

2 oz Vodka or Gin
1oz dry vermouth
1 dash of orange bitters
Shaken or stirred

I left Hawaii and landed in Los Angeles. I chose Los Angeles because of my occupation – knowing that it would be so easy to find work there. I was, after all, still a traveling bartender. My life had meaning, and I lived it intentionally, yet I still felt the freedom to move about or just pick up, leave, and go wherever I wanted. I didn't care or even stop to think what other people thought about my life or my choices. To some people, I'm sure that my actions may have seemed irresponsible or impetuous, but I truly didn't care. What mattered to me is that those closest to me, my friends and family members who understood me, knew that I was just being myself – the butterfly – living freely.

As soon as I turned on my phone after landing from Hawaii, Sharon Davis, a friend of mine from VSU, just so happened to be in LA visiting her cousin. Sharon had a knack for texting me when I most needed to hear a word from God or just to uplift me, and this time she didn't disappoint. Chiquita Bazemore and Fahja Bey were others that would always text at the right time. They never knew that God used them in a manner that blessed me tremendously. I'm so grateful for them.

I visited Sharon at her cousin's house, and after meeting her cousin, she inspired me to do more of what I longed to do. I loved how she was a world traveler who would stay in hostels and just go. I wanted that lifestyle. I wanted that freedom. I loved her free spirit. Her cousin just so happened to be on her next adventure and was looking for a house sitter. I needed a place to complete my divorce paperwork, which was also delivered after I had landed. It was a good situation to be in. At that time, Sterling was in New Mexico still getting offers and scholarships to play football, so I needed to be closer to him. God was there in the midst of what some would consider confusion.

I stayed at her home for about ten days, enough time to finish my divorce paperwork. Her home was four blocks away from Santa Monica Beach and within walking distance of the infamous Santa Monica Pier. I enjoyed going to work every day. I was afforded the opportunity to catch beautiful sunsets and take long walks on the beach. People would say to me, "You came from all of this to nothing?" But I would say that, on the contrary, this has been a beautiful journey. There are two types of pain in this world – pain that hurts you and pain that changes you. I was so ready for change because I was being made over. I was becoming brand new.

Six months after our divorce, Jowell got remarried. He and I were best friends up until then. I was so happy for him. I expressed that to him in person, so he could see the purity in my heart. I am reminded of this song by Kamauu, entitled "Mango" which describes love as "never selfish" but "on purpose." Everyone deserves happiness. We were married until we weren't. It was that simple. We loved each other enough to let each other go. I accepted the fact that I was married to him for 30 years. After that, life goes on.

In LA, there was a 21-day gap until my friend's place would be available because I left Hawaii sooner than expected. The friend, who I first solicited to do my initial jump, and I reconnected since I did some jumps without him. He said I could come live with him when his place was ready, and I needed that time to readjust.

Sterling left New Mexico again due to academic struggles and decided to join the military. I was so thankful for that time that he was in basic training to allow myself to adjust. He excelled at basic training, and his first duty station was at Fort Lewis, Washington. The military has changed tremendously over the years. When Taylore was in The Coast Guard, I still had some familiarity of what I was accustomed to when I was a military wife. By the time Sterling joined the Army it was so different. I don't know if it was the Army that had changed or the people who were a part of it – or maybe it was me – I was different. I was thankful for Sterling joining the Army, because it was then we found out that he had some underlying health issues which explained why he was having so much trouble with education. By staying with my friend at the time, it afforded me the opportunity to go back and forth to ensure that he was getting the best medical care. He needed some assistance, and I rose to the occasion. Mothers always do. I had the lifestyle for it and I was happy to be there for my adult children. It helped that I was working as a traveling bartender so that I could fly back and forth.

Taylore was working with a major hotel brand, so again God gave me a lot of sweet moments. I was traveling and the accommodations, adventures, and views were beautiful. It was almost like having bittersweet moments on a daily basis. I was getting messages from a lot of people who were inspired by my journey, but they didn't really know about my journey. While you're an active participant in life, you don't realize the whole picture either. I was a mother who had one child who had a traumatic experience as a teenager, and now found out that I had another with a learning disability. All of this falls under the umbrella of Mental Health. I didn't realize it at the time, because when you're constantly skipping, leaping, and jumping, you don't see that God has been an umbrella of protection during the whole process. His provisions for me and my children have been full of love and protection. He made my journey attractive and adventurous. He opened my eyes to learning how to lean on His promises. That's what faith looks like. I was being rewarded with traveling and meeting new people daily. I was growing and learning. My eyes were open to new things and experiences and that's what was attracting people to my journey – my creator. I developed all of this from taking a leap and never going back to what my norm was.

Dr. Jamal Bryant once said, "You can't run from a mountain that you were born to climb," and little did I know that's what I was about to experience. They say it takes 21 days to break a habit, and for 21 days I had a job but no shelter. My friend at the time, who I planned to stay with, had a home that was not going to be ready for 21 days. With no place to go, my spirit could have been broken. I listened again to Steve Harvey's story and almost every story of anyone who had experienced hardships after deciding to live a life they wanted. I decided this time I would utilize my money differently and decided to sleep in my car at night. All I knew is that God works the night shift!

I did not spend one sleepless night during those 21 days. The money I was making daily, I used for my health. I would get massages, go to the gym on the military base and sit in the sauna. I would shower after my workout and go to the beach twice a day. I ministered to other homeless people, donated food and money, and saw the beauty in everyone. The people at Santa Monica Beach knew my schedule and again, I was surrounded by people who just wanted to be around me. I offered them hope and led some to Christ. I felt like Job from the Bible – everything that the enemy threw at me, God protected me from.

I am so thankful for living out loud because the messages and calls I received gave me life. God ministered to me as I ministered to others. It was an ebb and flow, like the ocean. When we realize that all our troubles are always in front of us, we see them, feel them, and experience them daily. I truly felt as if God's "goodness and mercy were following me" every day.

I was walking with purpose and have now collided with destiny. I went from having what some would think was a good life to having nothing. After I counted the things money can't buy, I realized I was right where I needed to be.

For those 21 days, I can't put into words what I experienced because I think some experiences are just for you. It was another life-changing experience. I thought I was free until I saw what true freedom is like. I sat and broke bread with people who didn't have shelter, but they had jobs and dreams. I met people like me that were meant to be free. I had the opportunity to give and receive. I was receiving knowledge from people from all walks of life and was in total awe.

I met a gentleman from Ibiza, Spain, who approached me and said he was told to serenade me with a song. I had no idea what the words were, but I do know music in any language is healing to your spirit. I was thankful for having previously lived in Europe. I was able to talk and relate to everyone I met, and even brushed up on my German with another person there. People came from all over the world to California to live out the American dream and pursue happiness. It reminded me so much of movies I'd seen because L.A. is the city of dreams, and the people I met were literally those who gave up everything to pursue happiness. California is filled with these types of people.

I realized that I also inspired a kind of wanderlust in people who admired what I was doing and took the time to tell me so via their text messages and social media exchanges. I often wondered if those people would still admire my journey if they knew that I was homeless, but I never felt ashamed about it.

Never. Instead, I felt inspired by those life-changing 21 days. I knew that God would use my mess and turn it into a miracle. In the words of Eckhart Tolle, "Some changes look negative on the surface but you will soon realize that space is being created in your life for something new to emerge."

It was me; I was new – like the butterfly. I'd become a new person. It was so fun to be a traveling bartender. I met so many interesting and famous people because I attached myself to a catering company that had high-profile jobs that allowed me to be around them and work in Hollywood as well. I met the late Kobe Bryant, Dennis Rodman, Steve Nash, and Ocho Cinco, just to name a few. Chad Ocho Cinco was so nice. I was working a VIP event in Long Beach at The Convention Center and he wouldn't let me take a picture of him. He said to me, "The only way you're getting a picture is if you're in it with me." He took my phone from my hand and snapped our photo. I was also grateful to meet some daytime actors who I grew up watching.

One day, I was driving in Newport Beach, California, when I had a sudden bout of vertigo. After leaving from getting acupuncture to help alleviate my symptoms, I saw Dennis Rodman driving by. I turned the car around on another adventure and lost him, or so I thought. I turned down a dead end to get back on track to where I was going, and there he was. I said to him, "Can I get a picture with you?" He held out his arms and said, "Come." He and I laughed and talked for about 5 minutes and even danced because he had music playing loudly in his car. And just like that, the adventure was over.

I also ran into Steve Nash in Playa Vista at Whole Foods. During the 21 days, I ate breakfast, lunch, and dinner there. Steve Nash and I talked about juicing. He ordered a green juice, and I had my regular juice. That Whole Foods location allowed you to buy food and take it to their cafe on-site, where the kitchen would cook it for you. Plus, they had a hot bar. I learned to pivot daily, and it fueled me. This helped me to become a Travel Agent and I immediately became my biggest customer. I craved new people, ideas, and ways. I was a sponge, and I was renewed by the energy of living in California. So many talented people will take their talents to their graves because they are fearful of change. I was not going to be one of them.

After the 21 life-changing days of sleeping in a car, I was stable. I then decided that I would explore all of California while I was there. I added the title of travel-video blogger/vlogger, as well as a travel bartender. I visited hotels throughout the state and experienced some perks from my new position. It was beneficial that I worked in the industry.

The experiences were fun and full of adventure. At times, I traveled by air, but it was traveling by land that was the most rewarding. It is there where you can see the heart of America and all of its beauty, even in ugly times. I know I have traveled thousands of miles all across the United States. I did theme trips. I experienced things that I would never be able to put into words. It was almost an exchange. I had to endure hardship for 21 days, but what I received was exactly what I wanted and needed. Was it different from what I knew my whole life? Yes, because I had never been homeless – but I also have never felt that alive and full of purpose and freedom. My life has always been sweet and sour, joy and pain, and I continued to have those experiences. I worked hard and played even harder.

Did Taylore and Sterling require my attention? Yes. Was I able to jump, skip, and leap whenever they needed me? Yes! Most of all, I wanted for them to be stable. They always had their own places and as their mother, I would come to them and tend to their needs. Sterling finally gave up his dream of playing football and Taylore was thriving despite the ups and downs of life. She is naturally smart and wise beyond her years.

I was able to assist my children in a capacity that I would not have been able to before emotionally and spiritually, especially if I had a full-time job that wasn't flexible. What I have learned is when young adults go through traumatic experiences, it causes some memory loss, according to The Mayo Clinic. One study suggests that survivors of traumatic incidents are sometimes at the same age as when their trauma happened.

However, on her website, *The Best Medicine for Humans is Love*, Dr. Michelle Robin quotes an unknown author who states the following: "A wise physician said, 'The best medicine for humans is love.' Someone asked, 'If it doesn't work?' He smiled and answered, 'Increase the dose.'" And with each skip, leap and jump, that's exactly what I did for myself and my children.

Eventually, I moved to South-Central L.A. I didn't realize it wasn't a desirable place. I had given back everything in my divorce, including my car so I learned how to get around through public transportation. It seemed as though you could get around faster there without one anyway. I was full of life and happy. I felt purpose. I was living, exploring, and growing.

In all the things I was going through, I learned and leaned on God. I realized that what got me through all that I had been through was grace– specifically because of the grace that had been extended to me. My soul was so thankful for that. I was going to the ocean daily, and watching the West Coast sunsets renewed my spirit so that I was able to offer hope to anyone that wanted it. Spending time with nature in the beauty of God's creation always allowed me to refuel, and in turn, that allowed me to be there for my children. It is a standing joke between my children and I – I call them Chicken Littles, a cartoon character, who always went around telling people the sky was falling. So now when they call, my question to them is, "Is the sky really falling? Do you really need me or is it a want?"

In the words of David Viscott, "The meaning of life is to find your gift. The purpose of life is to give it away." My past will never dictate who I am. It serves as a lesson that will strengthen the person I am still becoming. The richness of my experiences and the people I've met are worth documenting in words. They mean too much to me not to do it. I realized not too far into my journey that other people may feel grounded, stuck, unhappy, unfulfilled, and just frustrated or exhausted with the weight of other people's expectations, or the situations they have found themselves in and feel like they don't have options. Let me be the first to tell you that your ability to jump, leap, and skip will always bring fresh energy and perspective and offer a reward to you mentally and spiritually, even if you don't know it yet.

Some may say, "Why would I want to go through all of the bad just to get to the good? Isn't normalcy better?" No! In the words of Vincent van Gogh, "Normality is a paved road where no flowers grow." I say that it's also like making fresh-squeezed lemonade. Lemons by themselves are bitter or sour. Those are the rough patches in your life. Water is your soul's spiritual growth and connection – it is also essential for survival. We all know that our bodies are made of 75% water which is vital to our existence as humans. But, the final ingredient in lemonade is sugar. The sugar or sweetener is God's grace and mercy – that sweetness that is catered especially for you. That's how the best lemonade in the world is made. We all are dealt a measure of faith, and I'm so thankful that God knew He could trust me to share that. Even through the storms of life, He is always an umbrella. I was graced for everything I've been through. We take risks daily. Why not be intentional with our risk? To risk is to live.

This has been a never-ending journey filled with the highest of highs and the lowest of lows. I still count it all as joy since I'm here and better for every bumpy landing and rocky shoreline. I have come to see that life itself is a miracle. Your priority should be to not waste a second of your miracle on your pain, whatever it is. A disappointment in not having your life turn out as you wanted, or experiencing the loss of someone you love, can bring about tremendous pain. Nevertheless, I woke up every day grateful that God somehow gave me the strength to displace that pain and move on toward my purpose. Even if I had thrown in the towel and gone back home, I would have been nurtured and saved. However, I wouldn't have grown and learned to trust and minister to others as I have on my own, nor would I have this wonderful testimony of leaping forward.

As I let go, the jumps allowed me to rely on God even more, which increased my faith. That gave me the energy and optimism to create a new reality from what remained – or what I was given – to form a new and purposeful life with what I had. As believers in God, we will arrange our lives. We all can relate to that. It won't always be easy, but I believe that having the courage to take the steps you need to take and move – whether it's a jump, a skip, or a leap - will help you get that much closer to your purpose.

This story is a very small part of my life but I hope it helps someone. I encourage you to listen to your heart, take the leap of faith, and know that even in setbacks, there is always room for a comeback. As you prepare for future jumps, I know you may be reluctant because once you jump, you're not grounded anymore. That can be a very fearful feeling, but in reality, you are allowing God's guidance. You are putting your faith in Him. You can't fail. The freedom you gain from it is a feeling that you have never experienced. It's a feeling of vulnerability, but also safety. That's what jumps are all about - FAITH. Knowing that if you don't end up where you want to be, you are right where you should be. Don't be afraid of taking chances. As my father said, it's a "win-win situation." You will learn something new. In the words of Kenji Miyazawa, "We must embrace pain and use it as fuel for our journey."

This has been the worst and best experience of my life. As I've experienced my jumps, I've morphed into a butterfly and a storyteller. I'm still living, learning, and leaning on God and I trust those journeys that have yet to unfold and have something important to teach me. I'm starting over from experience and choosing what and who I want to be. I can't explain how I've had an abundant void of material things. I'm different but also fundamentally the same person – shaped by my life's experiences.

This book ends in Los Angeles, but I plan to keep jumping. God put an exclamation point on the ending of this chapter of my life. During the pandemic, Taylore, Sterling, and I all reconnected in one house. Of course, we didn't know the pandemic was coming. We were going to Texas to help Taylore move into her new apartment. She received a promotion, and Sterling had just gotten out of the Army. Two weeks after arriving in Texas, the world shut down. I am so thankful that we were all together. God knew I would have lost my mind if I couldn't have gotten to one of my children, had they needed me. One day while at one of Sterling's V.A. appointments, a man approached him and asked him if he played football. Sterling told him he did. He asked if he would be interested in officiating. Sterling wasn't interested but gave the man his information. Football season was almost over, and his love for football had vanished. He stopped watching football after his failed dream and forgot all about the conversation. About a year later, I reminded him of the man and the conversation they had. Sterling couldn't remember the man's name. Two weeks after I asked, the man contacted Sterling, and he's back on the field again with the game he grew up playing. He is officiating Texas Friday Night Lights!

During the season, football is played every day in Texas. During his rookie year, he has already been asked to officiate at the collegiate level for next season. He also has an activewear clothing line called *Love Seoul*, in honor of his late paternal grandmother, Chong Sue Young-Parks, and his father, who were both born in Seoul, Korea. Taylore is a governmental contractor and is also a business owner, who uses her knowledge of herbs to aid in women's health and wellness. Since her accident, she has been on a never-ending journey of healing through homeopathic remedies. She is so skilled. I've been trying to close out California and make my way back east and for whatever reason, that's not where I'm meant to be. I now reside between California and Las Vegas, living my life on my own terms. I do resort living, because I still long for warm weather and never-ending vacations. I work with homeless programs in L.A., and wherever I skip, leap, or jump to, that is what I will continue to do. I've given up bartending and my name, The Sunset Bartender. My life has taken me into new territory, and I've developed a closer walk with my creator. I am a travel agent and a travel vlogger. Also, I am currently a Certified Life Coach and Motivational Speaker and I look forward to using my life's journey to show others how they can fail forward while not being afraid of failing. I knew I needed to document this chapter of my life early after landing, because the truth sometimes is unbelievable. I'm so happy and humbled not only to share it, but to turn the page on this chapter of my life. The freedom I've gained from it is priceless, and I will forever cherish every moment of it. Every day we are blessed to awaken is proof that we are here for a purpose. If you are feeling like you are in need of change, then you have to believe that something greater is coming. You mustn't ever be afraid to launch into the deep and skip, leap, or jump because "*The ugly part of your story will become the most powerful part of your testimony.*"

Here's to those of us who will make the JUMP and live life FOR LIVING!!!

St. Germain Champagne Cocktail

1 oz St. Germain

1 oz Gin

½ oz Lemon Juice

½ Maple Syrup

3 oz Champagne

Rosemary twig

Shaken

Final Reflections

Do you really know what you were born to do? If so, what's hindering you from doing it?

If not, think about it and make a list below of the things you feel aren't working and the things that make you happy and smile.

IT'S YOUR TURN TO JUMP!!!

ACKNOWLEDGEMENTS

"When you have people who root for you, it makes you stronger. "Thank you...

My Sisters	Daryl Kelson
LaRonda Montiero-Tuckson	James Henderson
Dr. Michelle Pegram	Shauna Morris
Keturah Brown	Harvey Holloway
Fahja Bey	Monica Taylor
Stacey Fitzgerald-Redd	Clarence Walker
Keith Copeland	Moniquie Acosta-House
Chiquita Bazemore	Tracey Chiles-McGhee
Kimberly Woodard	Cynthia Sailor
Samantha Robinson	Michelle Warren
Jill Stokes	Aliesia White-Davis
Sandra Butler	Adreena Martin
Dr. Kathy Frazier	Kelos Riggins

Tobey A. Jackson Martin ▶ **Freetobeme L'Tanya** ⋯

Apr 18, 2016 · ⚙

I wish you the best on this next chapter! You will succeed!

"Forget everything you've done. Start over."
— Marty Rubin

MAR 01, 8:14 AM

 I wanted to reach out this morning and say I love you!! You are strong and courageous! Believe me your walk through this life is a testimony of God's favor!

MAR 01, 9:01 AM

I am so thankful to God for you!! Thank you so much! All I want is to walk in HIS Glory! Love you more

About the Author

L'Tanya Parks is an entrepreneur, travel blogger, motivational speaker, Life Coach, and free spirit. Her life's mission is to chase the most beautiful sunsets and discover peace and renewal near the ocean and on the beaches of the world and to instill in others that FAITH doesn't always make sense, but it makes room for miracles. She is the mother of two children, Taylore and Sterling Parks.

From Sterling Parks:

My Mom is an Entrepreneur by day and Superwoman by night. You are the reason I'm still alive and I'm so proud of you for telling your story as only you could. I'm so grateful that you live in your purpose and inspire others to live in theirs. You have an eye for beautiful sunsets and will pull a car over to gaze at one. You have taught me so much, but most importantly, that it is never too late to find your purpose.

From Taylore Parks

Mom, you are fierce and fearless, and you never cease to amaze me. You have such a love for life, travel, family, friends, sunsets, and beaches. Your greatest gift is the ability to nurture and inspire everyone you meet, and all are warmed by your free spirit and courage. What I love most about you is that you are unapologetically yourself and live your life fully, without concern about the scrutiny of other people. You continue to be an inspiration and a gem, and I know that everyone who reads your story will love you as much as I do.